AUSTRALIA

that w

Cheer a Chook

PHILIP R. RUSH

To my wife Yvonne, for her labour of love in reading every poem I write and giving both her valued criticism and encouragement.

To Viv Roberts for her time and expertise in editing; a most generous gift.

To Heather Bond, for her typing skills, patience and cheerful endeavour.

And to all my readers - an enormous thank you!!

By the same author

Bess, The Black Orpington Swaggie
Australian Poems That Would Stun A Sheep
More Than Nine Lives
Australian Poems That Would Boggle A Bull
Tales from Mosquito Gully and Other Australian Poems
Australian Poems that would Flummox a Farmer
Aussie Poems for Gnome and Garden
Australian Poems that would Dazzle a Dingo
Australian High Country Poems
Australian Outback Poems
Australian Wildlife Poems
Australian Poems That Would Baffle a Bandicoot
Australian Poems That Would Captivate a Koala
Australian Poems That Would Humour a Horse

Published by Philip R. Rush Pty. Ltd. A.C.N. 082 969 882
224 Sunny Hills Road
Glen Huon Tasmania 7109
www.philiprush.com.au

1st Edition August 2006 2500 copies

Printed and bound by The Monotone Art Printers Pty Ltd.
Argyle Street, Hobart Tasmania

ISBN 0-9758134-1-2

CONTENTS

JACK OF ALL TRADES

(The fact that so many farmers have a multitude of skills never ceases to impress me. From welding to mechanical repairs, from building to shearing, from fencing to plumbing, so many of them can do it all!)

Old Jim lives on a farm nowadays and runs it pretty well,
Producing on his property both wheat and wool to sell.
And since he has a lot of help from both his son and wife,
They have, in comfort and in style, a rather pleasant life!

But Jim's not always owned a farm, he's had it pretty rough;
In fact, for more than twenty years his life was hard and tough!
He worked on stations near and far for years as shearers' cook;
And even as a tarboy once when things were really crook!

He's been a drover, too, at times, on stock routes everywhere.
Of restless stock and flooding creeks he's more than had his share.
He worked as ringer way out west along the famed Barcoo;
And worked as fettler on the rail, and as a jackeroo.

There's nothing in the farming line that old Jim hasn't done;
And all his skills and expertise he's passed on to his son.
Shearing, droving, fencing, and how to ride a horse;
And how to work machinery, and fix it, too, of course!

He'd always wished to own a place, give settled life a try;
It took him nearly thirty years to save enough to buy
An undeveloped piece of land - you wouldn't know it now,
He's made it quite the model farm through nous and sweat of
brow.

He's close to seventy years of age, and weather-beaten, too,
He looks you squarely in the eye each time he speaks to you!
He seems to some a little gruff, some say a trifle cold;
But he will always help a mate; he has a heart of gold!

"Just where is old Jim's house and farm?" Well, I can't tell you that;
It's where so many folk call home, the place they hang their hat.
For Jim is a generic bloke who's had a lot to bear;
The unsung battler in our land, you'll find him everywhere!

WINTER FIRES

(One of the great joys of life is sitting by a fire on a cold winter's night. Here in Tasmania our house needs heating for six to seven months of the year, and the wood-fired heaters we have in the house do the job marvellously!)

I lit the fires last Friday for the day was pretty chill,
And I reckon they'll stay burning for several months until
Sometime in late September when spring's well under way,
When we may decide to let them die down throughout the day.
But we could easily need them to still be burning bright
As cool October evenings change to cold October nights!

You come straight into the kitchen when visiting our place,
Where a slow-combustion stove fills up a corner space.
We keep it operating almost all the year through,
For it gives us our hot water, and very cheaply, too!
It can be rather messy, but that's the price we pay
For the pleasant warmth it gives us and hot water every day.

If I wake up in the morning to a raging winter storm,
It doesn't bother me a bit, the house is always warm!
For the fires are both still burning, as they've been throughout the night,
And to see the flames still flickering is a very pleasant sight!
The only downside to it is my dwindling stack of wood,
For I rarely keep the woodshed quite as full as, perhaps, I should!

TO THE PEOPLE OF BALI

(After the horror and destruction of the terrorist bombing in Bali, a group of people in the little Tasmanian town of Cygnet organised a special day to raise money for the many Balinese who had suffered so much both during and after that terrible day. They asked me to write a poem for the occasion, and this is it.)

We have a favourite playground, an island where we go
To have a rest, and just relax, where life is rather slow.
Where folk are always friendly, they greet you with a smile;
And always have sufficient time to stop and chat a while.

But even on vacation we tend to rush about,
Relaxation isn't easy; the stress of work, no doubt.
But don't make haste in Bali, that paradise sublime,
They'll tell you, "palin, palin, - slow down and take your time!"

The island is idyllic, where all is lush and green,
With softly swaying palm trees, and beaches quite supreme.
Where surf and sand together, beneath a tropic sky,
Present a glorious picture, a pleasure to the eye.

The people, too, are marvellous, a gentle, loving race,
They're all so kind and friendly, and have a certain grace.
They make you feel so welcome, you really feel at home;
No folk you'll find more pleasant, no matter where you roam!

They're not a wealthy people, but tourists, when they come,
Provide a living for them, but not a princely sum.
Their economy is fragile, they're in a lot of strife
If the tourist dollar's lacking, for it's their way of life!

But now this tropic Eden, this Shangri-la today
Has felt the blaze of terror in a most horrific way.
Their world has been up-ended, their innocence is lost;
The bombs of mid-October brought a massive, brutal cost.

We lost our sons and daughters, we lost our parents, too,
We lost our friends and neighbours, we lost someone we knew.
We've grieved and wept and sorrowed, we've tried to understand
Why there are those who savage the people of our land.

We've tried to help the suffering, we're mourning with them still,
And wonder at the mindset of those who maim and kill.
We struggle to imagine the maniacal force
That delights to leave destruction and terror in its course.

I haven't got an answer, and, maybe, nor have you,
But we don't need an answer to know what we can do.
We have no need of violence, that doesn't solve a thing,
But we can show our caring, compassion we can bring.

We may, down here in Tassie, say it won't happen here,
And live in isolation, knowing we've not much to fear.
We must not let fanatics our peace of mind destroy,
We must not let the terrorists take away our joy.

We must not build a wall around our nation, rich and free,
But look to help our neighbours who live across the sea.
For we're a global village, the earth is ours to share,
So, wherever folk are hurting, we need to show we care.

So what about the island, and the gentle Balinese?
We're dealing with our loved ones, but not folk overseas.
The utter devastation that the islanders have felt
Is ever with them daily, it's seen and heard and smelt.

There're families now in crisis, they're struggling day to day,
For husbands, wives and children were simply blown away!
And jobs, of course, are lacking, with all the tourists gone,
And they've no social service for them to live upon.

The Balinese are precious, they've been Australia's friends
For very many years now, can we our hands extend
And help them in their troubles, to offer them some hope,
To make some contribution so the families can cope?

So what, I hear you asking, can a person such as me,
Do for Balinese from Tassie? It's not easy, I agree.
We can make a cash donation, and suggest it to a friend,
We can lobby for our Government some further aid to send.

I'm sure, that if we bother, there's much that we can do
For anyone we know in need, both here and Bali, too!
Let's choose to love our neighbour; and I, for one, believe,
That it is always better to give than to receive!

TO THE GRANDPARENTS

(I wrote this poem and then presented it to the illustrator of many of my books, Syd Woon, and his wife, Marie, on the birth of their first grandchild.)

What's it like to be a granny? What's it like to be a pa?
I can tell you it's exciting - grandkids think you are a star!
When the first grandson or daughter arrives both fit and strong,
It can be overwhelming when the waiting has been long!

I know it makes one realise that we must be getting old,
When another generation joins the growing family fold.
And, although we love the kiddies, it is plain for us to see
That it's best our children raise them, not the likes of you and me!

We've had our turn at rearing when we were in our prime,
But our bodies and our energy have felt the weight of time.
We love to see our grandkids, hear them 'goo' and watch their
smile,
But it's good we can return them when we've had them for a while!

"I'm not good with little children." Well, I've heard that one before,
From a certain ageing gentleman. I'll tell you this, for sure;
You'll be a hit with children that will call you Pa or Gramps,
And they'll leave you more exhausted than your monthly country
tramps!

And Granny, you'll feel different, and a little teary-eyed,
But you'll show the latest photos with a proper sense of pride!
You'll notice things, when shopping, that you haven't seen for years,
And buy the cutest items - "Just for the little dears!"

It's hard when family leaves us, and travels far away,
But I'm convinced that, somehow, on a not too-distant day,
There'll be a sweet reunion, and the tiny tot you'll hold,
More valuable than diamonds, or than the finest gold!

I suppose you'll both be busy, maybe making clothes and toys
That can be worn or played with by little girls or boys!
Your grandchild's very lucky to have the likes of you,
Two wonderful grandparents, both very clever, too!

When toddlers come to visit, we re-arrange the place,
The breakables on ledges are lifted - just in case!
But still we love to have them, to share their laughs and tears,
(Even if their little fingers cover everything with smears!)

I'm told they make us young again - I guess for some that's true,
It didn't seem to work for me - but, p'raps, it might for you!
I can see you playing cricket with a reckless four-year-old,
And looking quite astonished at being well and truly bowled!

Or maybe it is netball, or to tennis they're inclined,
But, whatever is the sport they play, they leave us well behind!
Their skills are soon superior, they think they are the best!
And they never understand it when you need to take a rest!

So congratulations, Granny! Congratulations, Pa!
A celebration's warranted, so here's hip, hip hoorah!
You've waited many years for this - your joy is plain to see!
So here's to yours and baby's health - I'll drink to you with tea!!!

FISHING

(Fishing is not one of my favourite activities, yet I have fished in many places, as this poem relates. But I have not fished in Tasmania, certainly one of the best trout-fishing spots in the world!)

I've fished the Wimmera River just below the Antwerp Weir,
And caught a hundred redfin without any special gear
Except a baltic bobber on a simple fishing line,
I went there after school one day with teacher friends of mine.

I spearfished in Port Phillip Bay some fifty years ago,
I used a hand spear I had made ten feet long or so.
Flathead, flounder, stingray, sole, and leatherjacket, too,
We speared quite often on the reefs and sandbars we each knew.

And in the vast Pacific I've fished for yellow fin,
And kingfish, too, and trumpeter, just simply hauled them in!
'Twas Norfolk Island where I fished some three miles off the coast,
"Best fishing you'll find anywhere," was always Norfolk's boast.

I haven't fished for forty years, though they're a favourite meal,
I find that buying fish and chips is now the better deal!
And as for Tassie's inland lakes, as you have guessed, no doubt,
I've never fished on them at all, and never caught a trout!

THE RECORDER

(Recorders - I have many of them! I have always enjoyed playing them, and still do. I also introduced many schoolchildren to the joys of the recorder, and taught many of them to play.)

'All maids that make trial of a Lute or a Viol…
If you like not this Order, come try my recorder.'

(D'Urfey *Pills…1719)*

'A wind instrument of the flute or flageolet kind.'

(OED – 2nd Edition).

'One of them plaied on a Lute; another on a Harpe; another made a maruellous sweet countertenour vpon a Recorder.'

(Yong *Diana)*

'The popularity of the instrument spread in the twentieth century after its revival by Arnold Dolmetsch in 1919.'

(OED – 2nd edition)

'The present-day meteoric return to popularity of the recorder – whose seductive tone charmed the ears of Henry VIII , Shakespeare and Pepys— is a development unparalleled in the history of any other musical instrument.'

(E.Hunt *—Recorder and its Music 1962)*

A wooden pipe with wondrous tone,
Played in a group or on its own.
Like every instrument we play,
It shouldn't see the light of day
Or heard in public place until
It's played with goodly grace and skill.

Recorders hold a few surprises,
And come, of course, in various sizes.
From tiny sopranino mites,
To 'grossbass"– an impressive sight!
They come in wood, and plastic, too,
And some can cost a bob or two!

Recorders, ancient instruments of old,
Great to feel, to play, to hold.
Pear wood, maple, walnut, beech,
Are used, but ebony is out of reach
For most, for their cost is high,
Too much for many folk to buy!

A blackwood bass, you understand,
Can set you back some twenty grand!
But plastic descant ones, I guess,
Will cost five dollars, sometimes less!
And great they are for kids to play
Some music in our schools today!

Like chocolates or some sticky bun,
I'm not content with only one.
I love the sound, the shape, the wood,
Of those I have, and if I could
I'd like to add a dozen more
To the twelve I have in store!

THE SPOT IS ALWAYS ON THE OTHER SIDE

(Self-explanatory!)

I had polished all the floors,
And the brass knobs on the doors,
And removed the cobwebs off the walls outside.
Then I made a pot of tea,
Put a book upon my knee;
For my cleaning left me very satisfied.

But before I read my book,
I chanced to take a look
At some birds upon the apple tree outside.
On the window there I saw,
A spot I'd missed before;
But the wretched spot was on the other side!

So outside I quickly went,
For I wouldn't be content
Until I'd wiped that dirty spot away!
But as I wiped it clean,
Another spot was seen!
On the other side this time, to my dismay!

I'd not noticed it before,
The mark on auntie's jaw,
On her photo I was happening to pass.
I tried earlier today
To wipe the mark away;
But the spot was on the inside of the glass!

I may sound a little terse,
But I find there's nothing worse
Than cleaning windows, and once the glass has dried,
Seeing dirty spots again
On every window pane!
And those spots are always on the other side!

DAISY

(A typical Jack Russell terrier! I know, we've owned a number of them!)

I was somewhat interested,
When recently requested
To write of a Jack Russell that's owned by someone here.
Like all Jack Russells, Daisy
Is intelligent and crazy;
And, like all her breed, courageous, devoid of any fear!

Though small in size and stature,
She thinks nothing else can match her,
So potential threats and enemies she'll tackle with a will.
She's a solid ball of muscle,
All huff and puff and bustle,
And you'll find, except when sleeping, she's hardly ever still.

One of her favourite habits
Is chasing all the rabbits
That are really rather numerous around her owner's place.
It's rarely she can catch them,
For, in speed, she cannot match them
And she finds it quite a mystery when they vanish without trace.

Until recently, a warren
Was, to her, completely foreign;
And how the rabbits disappeared was a puzzlement to her.
So this cheery little sinner
Missed every rabbit dinner,
She never even managed to get teeth into their fur!

But success came unexpected
Just last week, when she connected
The warrens in the paddock with the disappearing pests.
So last week she chose to follow
The rabbits down the burrows,
And there she stayed all evening, leaving owner unimpressed!

For her owner was quite frantic
At the disappearing antics
Of her favourite pet dog, Daisy, who was nowhere to be found.
She had vanished without warning,
And it wasn't until morning
That her mistress came to realise she might well be underground!

She found where she was hiding,
But no amount of chiding,
Would bring Daisy to the surface, she was having too much fun!
And it was ruefully conceded
That a shovel, then, was needed;
They'd have to dig the dog out in the morning's summer sun!

Once Daisy was discovered
She was laboriously uncovered
From her rabbit warren heaven with much vexation, toil and sweat!
Now my memory's somewhat hazy,
As what happened next to Daisy,
But her owner was not happy with her disappearing pet!

SIXTY YEARS AGO

(I was but a little lad sixty years ago. And it was sixty years prior to my writing this poem that the 'Country Hour' was first broadcast on ABC Radio in Australia. Six decades on, and it is still a much listened-to daily programme, especially by the rural community.)

The newspapers cost twopence back in nineteen forty-five,
And our prisoners of war returned, each pleased to be alive.
"Tarzan and the Amazons" was at the local flicks,
With Johnny Weismuller, of course, up to his usual tricks!
A refrigerator still, for us, was several years away;
The ice man brought the ice to us on every second day.
For washing, we'd a copper, Mum used Velvet soap, I think,
And Dad used for writing letters a dip-in pen, and ink.

There was no television, and computers were unknown!
There were manual exchanges when you used the telephone.
The milkman still delivered, and the baker did, of course,
As did the butcher once a week, all used a cart and horse!
For each evening's entertainment, once our homework had been
done,
We'd play dominoes, or ludo, or other games of fun!
And thirty cows would be enough for dairy farmers then,
And thirty bob, with bed and board, was paid to labouring men.

Don Bradman still played cricket, and still made massive scores,
The Second World War finished, they said there'd be no more!
The little Fergy tractor was seen upon the farm,
And, though it was extremely basic, it had a certain charm!
So much of what I've mentioned are things of yesterday,
And many won't be seen again, they've vanished right away!
Yet going strong for sixty years, an icon, you'd agree!
We still have our own 'Country Hour' upon the ABC!

UYAL CINEMA
AN and The
AMAZONS
TODAY
THE
ADVERTIS
Prime Minister
Welcomes
Prisoners
War
RALD

TO A CHOCOLATE ECLAIR

(The secretary at Glen Huon Primary School, where I spent many enjoyable days relief teaching from 1994 to 2001, is Lyn Bender. She has been a wonderful secretary of the school for over thirty years, as many will attest. She is also an excellent cook and makes the most delicious chocolate eclairs. These she often shares with the staff and, on this particular day, she telephoned me at home to say she had made some eclairs, and would be happy for me to drive the three kilometres down the hill to pick one up. This I did, and brought it home for morning tea - and I wrote this poem about it!)

I sit and I stare
At the chocolate eclair
That enticingly rests on my plate.
And, Oh! How unfair
That this chocolate eclair
When eaten, will add to my weight!

I don't really care
For an apple or pear;
Dry biscuits and I don't relate.
So I watch the eclair
As I sit in my chair,
And have an internal debate.

"Perhaps I should share
This chocolate eclair
With my daughter, my wife, or my mate."
I continue to stare
At this chocolate eclair,
And, Oh! The temptation is great!

I should really beware
Of cholesterol scare -
Was it seven point seven, or eight?
But is one eclair
That waits for me there,
Going to ultimately alter my fate?

"No way!" I declare;
And I really can't bear
To leave this delight on the plate.
So, at last, I prepare
To eat the eclair -
I'm convinced that my diet can wait.

Not a morsel I share,
As I eat it with flair;
The taste, and the flavour are great!
No cake can compare
With the luscious eclair
That, early this morning, I ate!

PORT HOBART

(One could say that the port of Hobart is part of the central business district of that city. With Mount Wellington overlooking the magnificent harbour, the port is a delightful place for a relaxing stroll or a quiet rest on a seat by the one of the wharves. I had an hour or so to fill in late one afternoon and could not resist the urge to write this poem.)

There's a jumble of boats in the Hobart port,
With a mix of vessels of various sort.
Some visiting trawlers, a ketch or two,
And some cruising yachts just passing through.
A catamaran from the USA;
It's a naval ship painted dreary grey.

There's a bustle of folk on the wharf today,
Some fishermen coming, some going away.
There're children having a bit of fun,
And others enjoying the evening sun.
There're families sharing their fish and chips,
While others inspect the numerous ships.

There's a tranquil calm on the longest pier;
And I relish the peaceful atmosphere.
I sit on a step and I watch the sea,
As the wavelets murmur in harmony.
A flock of gulls flies lazily by,
As the sun sets red in the western sky.

The colours fade over Hobart Town.
As the twilight shades come slowly down.
I've enjoyed my hour on the wharf today,
But I leave my step and make my way
Past the sleeping yachts in the failing light,
And the sea breeze whispers a soft good night.

HAY CARTING AGAIN!

(Hay carting isn't my favourite occupation; especially since well passing the age where my body is no longer suited to such activity!)

It only seems a day or two
When I was talking hay to you.
And how it's many years since
I carted hay! It made me wince
Just to think of dust and heat
And making haystacks trim and neat.

But it was just the other day,
When I was on a mainland stay
With nephew, Brian, on his farm,
Who said, which caused me some alarm,
That he and Bradley, that's his son,
Had much hay carting to be done!

"You care to help?" he asked of me.
Well, I had no choice but to agree.
He'd got his ancient baler out,
And four thousand bales, or thereabout,
Of straw he'd baled in small square bales,
Which needed carting by we three males.

His tray truck was the way to go,
And loader, too, which, as you know,
Makes lifting easier for you,
But means you work much quicker, too.
Though bales of straw are fairly light,
The loader didn't have much height.

Two high was all that it could lift,
Which meant we fellows had to shift
The bales higher on the tray -
Six high in summer's heat that day!
And they'd be coming thick and fast;
It had been so long - so would I last?!

"Come on," he said. "We'd better start".
I thought about my ageing heart.
It's pretty good, and sound enough,
But did it need a workout tough?
But, pleased to say, I was in luck;
I only had to drive the truck!

THE WINTER OLYMPICS

(I was looking forward to watching the Winter Olympic Games on television. Just before they started, however, I had a poem to write for my regular weekly spot on radio and, since it was February the tenth, and I had no brilliant flash of inspiration, I wrote this!)

The Winter Olympics begin today in the northern Italian town
That is called Turin, and we hope this week the snow has been
plummeting down!
We've the biggest team that we've ever sent to a Winter Olympics
before;
We won some medals the last time round, this time we should win
some more!
Now today is the tenth, as you know full well, I did some research to
see,
What's happened on February ten before, what births and deaths
there be!
In eighteen forty a wedding there was, Queen Victoria married her
prince;
But no other royals have wedded this day, not ever before or since!

I'd never heard of Alanson Crane, but in eighteen sixty-three
The fire extinguisher he produced, and patented it, too, you see!
In nineteen ninety a Mr. De Klerk, from South Africa over the
way,
Announced that Nelson Mandela, at last, would be freed the
following day.
And the Voyager disaster occurred this day back in nineteen sixty-
four,
That's forty-two years, and some victims still, I believe, though I
can't be sure,
Have not yet received a brass razoo for the injuries they received;
No wonder that many throughout the years have been a trifle
aggrieved!
Robert Wagner, the actor, was born this day, and so was Roberta
Flack;
And Pope Leo the twelfth and Pius eleventh died this day, but many
years back!
And the first gold record for bumper sales, was awarded in forty-
two,
To Glenn Miller, it was, as we all know well, didn't make the world
war through.
Next year, I suppose, for many of us we'll see February the tenth
again;
But I doubt the history books will record, or any Internet page
explain
Why we were famous upon that day, but it surely won't bother me;
I'll be happy enough to survive that long, and another tenth of
February see!

PADDY'S CHRISTMAS

(This poem is partly based on a true story. Rural communities everywhere have been involved in similar situations right across our land. We still haven't lost the community spirit in such places.)

Paddy Thompson has some acreage beyond the thirteen mile;
And fate has been unkind to him, he's suffered many a trial;
But the toughest time he ever had was back in seventy-five
When Joan, his wife, was in a crash which she did not survive.

A drunken driver hit her car, drove into her, head-on!
She'd been his wife for twenty years, now suddenly was gone!
And Timothy, their only son, had trouble coping, too,
For once the funeral was held, the both of them withdrew.

Their friends and neighbours visited, but all were turned away,
As Paddy and his teenage son remained inside all day.
They neglected all the farm work, and the house was in a mess,
Which, considering the grief they'd had, was reasonable, I guess.

Eventually they did some work, which gave some slight relief
To Paddy Thompson and his son from endless days of grief;
But, as seasons came and seasons went, they led a hermit's life,
With Tim still grieving for his mum, and Paddy for his wife.

No joy they found in anything, their lives an endless grey;
Both miserable when shearing sheep, both gloomy cutting hay.
The locals left them well alone, for none were welcome there;
As Tim and Paddy struggled with depression and despair!

Tim went to town just once a week, and Paddy not at all;
And folk who telephoned would find they'd not return their call.
The farm fell into disrepair, the garden overgrown,
They even had a year or two where paddocks were unsown!

They lost a crop in eighty-two, or somewhere thereabout,
And, once again, in eighty-three, two years of wretched drought.
In eighty-four they tried again, at great financial strain,
But, thankfully, in early spring, they had some decent rain.

But still they lived reclusive lives, unhappy and morose;
They rarely spoke to anyone, and no-one could get close.
Their neighbour, Michael, sometimes came; they'd meet him at
the door;
And afterwards he'd wonder why he went there anymore!

It was only superficial chat that they would talk about;
A comment on the crops and stock, or rain or floods or drought.
He'd stand five minutes on the porch, they wouldn't ask him in;
And no matter what he said to them - they'd never smile or grin.

And then, in late September, disaster struck again!
A sudden storm approached the farm with driving wind and rain!
Both Tim and father Paddy were working in the shed,
And with the house five chain away, they sheltered there instead.

The sudden storm soon petered out but, with a final blow,
It tore the roof clear off the shed, and laid a gum tree low;
The tree fell down across the shed and hit both Dad and Tim,
Badly injuring them both, and things looked pretty grim!

Michael lived a mile away and, once the storm had gone,
He drove across to Paddy's place to see how they'd got on.
He saw the flattened tree and shed, he saw the tractor, too,
He thought the worst, and went across to see what he could do.

The men were pinned beneath the tree, and both had broken bones,
And Mike could hear the injured men give semiconscious groans.
Not only broken limbs they had, they both were badly crushed,
And both, once the alarm was raised, to hospital were rushed.

The doctors there did what they could, then called for further aid;
And, on further consultation, a decision then was made
A city hospital was best, for that was plain to see,
To get the treatment they required that's where they had to be!

So Michael came to visit them, and asked what he could do,
And Paddy gruffly said to him, "It'd help a bit if you
Could keep an eye on all the stock, and, perhaps, collect my mail."
Which, faithfully, his neighbour, Mike, did daily without fail.

"It's best to put the mail inside; here's the farmhouse key;
I think I left some switches on which you could check for me."
So Mike, his neighbour, went inside, and he was quite appalled;
No wonder that they talked outside when he on Paddy called!

Inside, the house was filthy, cobwebs nearly reached the floor;
Outside, the paint was peeling, and a hinge was off the door!
The garden was a jungle; paddock fences tired and slack;
And blackberries and other weeds were launching an attack!

When Mike told all the locals, they decided, one and all,
To gather for a meeting at the local, public hall.
And there they made a roster to fix up Paddy's farm,
To restore it how it used to be, with elegance and charm.

So almost eighty people volunteered their time that night,
To help at least two days a month, much to Mike's delight.
So every day for many weeks at Paddy's farm you'd see
Half a dozen locals working most harmoniously!

The ladies cleaned inside the house, they scrubbed the walls and floor;
Until each room was sparkling like they never had before!
They painted the exterior; reclaimed the garden, too:
The house and garden were revived, and looked brand, spanking new!

The men strained all the fences, they sprayed each noxious weed,
They saw the cattle, sheep and lambs all had sufficient feed.
They also did the shearing, they harvested the crop,
Not once, right up to Christmas, did the volunteering stop!

Meanwhile, both Tim and Paddy were completely unaware
Of what was happening on the farm, and who was helping there.
The injuries they had sustained were very slow to mend,
But the specialists were confident they'd get there in the end!

Both were in a deal of pain, and melancholy, too; and, as
Recovery progressed, their apprehension grew.
Their neighbour, Mike, was faithful, and visited each week,
But Tim and Paddy saw their future as nothing else but bleak!

They knew the stock was cared for, Mike had told them that;
But little else he told them when he came to have a chat!
At last the doctors told them they were well enough to leave;
"You can go home," they told them, "Next Monday, Christmas Eve."

Mike drove them home that morning, it took three hours or so
Before they drove in through the gate, and still they didn't know
What people had done for them - then, Oh! A huge surprise!
The farm looked postcard perfect, they scarce believed their eyes!

Two hundred folk were waiting to greet both Dad and Tim;
But Paddy wept, for what he saw was just too much for him!
When finally they left the car, the locals gave three cheers,
Which then affected Tim so much, he, too, was soon in tears!

The folk stayed for a barbecue, which they had all prepared,
A meal that Tim and Paddy both appreciatively shared.
And after all their neighbours left, they both went back inside,
And found their cupboards stocked with food, and, once again
    they cried.

Next morning they both went to church, for it was Christmas Day,
And Paddy stood and thanked them all - "I never can repay
The love and care you've shown us both, you've brought us life
    again;
And given to us both hope and joy, to ease our grief and pain."

Tim and his wife and children live in the house today,
And Paddy has a grandpa flat some sixty yards away.
But every year at Christmastide they have a barbecue
To which everyone's invited, including me and you!

FIRE PROTECTION

(A vital necessity in many places throughout Australia, Tasmania not being the least of them!)

Have you done your preparation for the season that's ahead?
Have you cleared the junk around your house, the junk around
your shed?
Have you cleaned the spouting recently? Got rid of all the leaves?
Have you filled in any gaps or holes you may have in your eaves?

The vegetation near your house - make sure you keep it short,
And check your pump and hoses, too, and other gear you've bought
To help protect from any fire that might flare up one day;
A lightning strike, or neighbour's burn that might have got away!

And, if it is appropriate, are all your firebreaks done?
Ploughed along the boundary fence, and paddocks, every one!
If told you have to leave your house, do you know what to do?
Have you prepared a safety plan for family and you?

It's raining here at home today, and everything is wet,
It's only mid-November, but how easy to forget
How quickly sun and wind can scorch, how quickly it can turn
From being green to being dry, when things can easily burn!

I've seen bushfires at their worst where mates of mine have died;
Each well-liked blokes in our brigade, and wept when families cried.
Get ready for the season now! Don't leave it all too late!
Remember - when the horse has bolted, it's no use to shut the gate!

SMITHS

HAYSTACKS!

(Haystacks! With the introduction of big round bales, and the subsequent reduction in small square ones, these once common sights in paddocks everywhere have now almost become a rarity! Yet I have mixed memories of them!)

A common sight for many years as I'm sure you're all aware,
Were well-constructed haystacks in paddocks everywhere.
Made up of small, rectangular bales I often used to cart;
They were, in many instances, a rural work of art!

The big, round bales we see today aren't any good for stacks,
And, by the way, there's not a bale that's any good for backs!
The smaller bales were just the thing for stacking in the shed,
Or, as we often used to see, in paddocks stacked instead!

You'd find in rural magazines, and books on farming, too,
Plans for stacking bales of hay, and things that one should do
To stop them overheating, and how to treat the hay
To stop them bursting into flame, and keep the mice away.

I helped build haystacks years ago for farmer friends of mine,
We'd build them in the paddocks to some approved design.
If slightly damp we'd salt them so they'd not overheat;
And each stack we constructed was stable, tight and neat.

One year we built a huge one of several thousand bales,
And made a wheat sack cover, with all that that entails!
It looked a little like a church, when ultimately done;
"Why don't you preach from on the top?" enquired the farmer's son.

"Yes, I guess I could," I answered, "But only on condition
That, next Sunday, you my lad should stand below and listen!"
"No way!" was his abrupt reply, "You'd preach too long, for sure!
And, besides, I'll need you then to help me cart some more!"

Haystacks like that are scarce today, as far as I can see,
And carting hay in century heat today is not for me.
But still I feel nostalgic about those haystacks still,
And faintly hear, while dreaming, "We'll cart tomorrow, Phil!"

TOO MUCH!

(We all know the old saying 'It's either a feast or a famine'. Here in Australia, this saying is often most applicable to rain, or lack of it!)

It's either feast or famine, it's either rain or drought!
This spring it is the rain's turn - even fence posts start to sprout!
The seeds of baby carrots are rotting in the soil,
And so are those of poppies, wasting weeks of farmers' toil!
I've heard that some potato crops are also rotting, too;
For they're water-saturated, and so am I - and you!

The ground up north's so waterlogged, I've heard some fellows say
They'll need some weeks of sun and wind before it drains away!
There're many can't get tractors in, they just get bogged in mud,
And hundreds of our Tassie towns this spring have seen a flood!
From St Helens down to Bicheno, from Gray to Deloraine,
We've seen flash flooding in the streets again, and yet again!

There're rainfall records broken all round this island State;
For some farmers it's meant trouble, for others it's been great!
For those of us dependent on water from our tanks,
We'd have to say these record rains have been received with thanks.
But we've had quite sufficient to meet all our summer needs,
I'm looking, now, for sunny days, and trust the rain recedes!

MY FAVOURITE SCHOOL EXCURSION!

(I think I was in grade five when we went on a school excursion to a very large working woolshed, an experience I have never forgotten, and one which gave me a strong desire to live in the bush when I was old enough to make up my own mind! And this I did!)

The shed was up and running when all of us arrived,
Thirty city schoolboys on a bus.
In suits and ties and purple caps, a consummate grade five;
About to witness something new to us!

Some fellow came to meet us, then ushered us inside
The biggest shed that we had ever seen!
The smell was overpowering, that cannot be denied;
Some boys were seen to turn a little green!

The noise was also different, a background buzz or whirr
Beneath the bangs and thumps and bleats and shouts.
It was all so loud and lively, the whole shed was a-stir,
It was hard to see what it was all about!

Then the bloke who came and met us showed us a quieter spot
Beside an open pair of wooden doors.
And in only fifteen minutes he explained to us the lot,
Then said that we could wander and explore.

"But don't go interfering! And don't interrupt the men!"
And he showed us where it was all right to go.
"Keep clear of the machinery! I won't tell you again!
But you will all behave your best, I know!"

Once the bloke had finished speaking, the teacher had a word,
Then up and down the shearing shed we went.
When I asked how big the shed was, "forty stand" I think I heard,
But I didn't understand just what he meant.

We'd arrived just after smoko, so we had an hour or more,
To discover what we could inside the shed.
And I was just enthralled by everything I heard and saw!
And today it's just as vivid in my head!

There were four wool-classing tables, and I think three presses, too,
And a row of open bins along the wall.
There were letters on each one of them, that's where the fellows threw
The fleeces, after classing, I recall.

I stood and watched the shearers, and I gazed at them in awe,
How quickly some of them removed the wool!
There was so much in that shearing shed that I'd not seen before!
And I never saw a shearer 'tear and pull'!

But I saw some sheep get injured, where the shearers cut the skin,
And heard the constant shouting out for tar!
I saw the tarboys with their buckets dip the stiffened brushes in;
And I'm sure some sheep would wear a nasty scar!

I stood beside the open doorway and gazed behind the shed,
Where ten thousand sheep were yarded, at a guess.
And I think the fellow told us they were all merino bred,
Yet of that I am not certain, I confess!

Though to us it looked chaotic, there was always order there,
And that order didn't happen just by chance!
For one fellow who was boss boy had his sharp eyes everywhere!
He'd pick up the slightest hiccup with his glance!

We heard the shed go silent when this boss boy rang the bell;
Well not completely quiet, as you know.
And so much more I can remember, but I haven't time to tell;
I nearly cried when we were told we had to go.

Now it's nearly sixty years since I saw that shearing shed;
A truly special memory of mine!
For no other shed I've been in, or ones of which I've read,
Can compare with what I saw in forty-nine!

HOME GARDENS

(I wrote this after reading a newspaper article extolling the value of a home vegetable garden. The writer of the article also spoke of the lengthy time many of our supermarket fruit and vegetables spend in storage before being put on sale!)

It was somewhat disconcerting when I read the other day,
That fruit and vegies in our shops so beautifully displayed
Aren't always fresh as we suppose - check it for yourselves -
For some are stored for many months before they're on the
shelves!

Some apples, so they tell me, and other fruits, as well,
Are sometimes stored a year or more, and how do shoppers tell?
And vegies, too, aren't what they seem; some gas is used, I'm told,
To keep them in a freshish state for weeks before they're sold!

No wonder some are weak and limp in just a day or two
From when we bought them from the shop, but what can
shoppers do?
Of course, there is an answer, as many folks have shown,
Dig up a patch of one's back lawn and try to grow your own!

My daughter has a lovely patch, as do our neighbours, too,
And we quite often did the same, fresh vegetables we grew.
We grew caulis and tomatoes, we grew lettuces and beans,
And no vegies from the shops can taste as fresh as garden greens!

My daughter's twins are only three, but great gardeners they are!
They water, weed, and pick the crops, the pride of Gran and Pa!
They know the name of what they grow, they treat them all with
care;
And it's proved a lovely pastime that the family can share!

They've carrots and tomatoes, they've grown lettuces and corn,
Parsley, mint and strawberries on their dug-up patch of lawn.
They dug up some potatoes which we had for Christmas dinner,
No matter how you look at it, their garden is a winner!

They've asparagus and rhubarb, they grow every kind of herb,
And the twins' enthusiasm and knowledge is superb!
They show you what is garlic, which are runner beans or chives,
And they know just what is needed to see each plant survives!

So if you are quite unhappy with the produce you can see
Displayed in supermarkets, then take a hint from me!
Enjoy some healthy exercise, dig up a patch of lawn;
And each of you may then enjoy fresh lettuces and corn!

EAT FRESH
VEG & FRUIT
CARROTS
½ Price
KENADEC
$1.50 kl

NOW THAT'S A WOOL CHEQUE!!

(It once used to be said that Australia's economy rode on the sheep's back. Wool was certainly Australia's most lucrative export for many decades, but not now. However, many can still remember the heady season of nineteen fifty/fifty-one when wool reached the incredible price of a pound a pound! This poem tries to give some idea of what this wool price means in modern-day terms!)

There are still a lot of farmers who can recall, I'm sure,
When greasy wool was worth a bit; when the Korean War
Was only in its infancy, and wool was in demand,
And reached an all-time record price that's hard to understand
In terms of values here today, so perhaps I should explain
How much its value really was, but never will again!

In season fifty/fifty-one, the average greasy price
Was one forty-four pence, more or less, I won't repeat it twice!
And that was just a pound of wool! Its equivalent today
In average weekly income terms, would blow you right away!
For in that time, since fifty-one, the average weekly wage
Has increased over fifty times, as far as I can gauge.

And so when just a pound of wool would cost one forty pence;
Today would be one thirty-three - in dollars, not in cents!
That's one thirty-three a kilogram, and so an average bale
Would sell for more than twenty grand at any normal sale!
A million bucks for forty bales!! That isn't quite the same
As what the farmer gets today - which really is a shame!

In nineteen fifty/fifty-one, as all the records tell,
Four sixty million pounds we earned from wool we had to sell!
That's export wool - and that would be in dollar terms today,
Adjusted for the CPI, twenty billion bucks, I'd say!
So 'Boonoke' with eighty thousand rams in nineteen forty-nine,
An eight-figure cheque they'd see today, and maybe even nine!

But those are cheques to dream about, no Rolls Royce could we buy
With wool at seven hundred cents, as all can testify.
Seven hundred cents a kilogram equates, if I'm correct,
To seven pence a pound back then, too little, I suspect!
Those heady days are gone for good - for, looking down the track,
Our economy won't ride again on our merino's back!

SUMMER VISITORS

(I have been a keen birdwatcher virtually all my life. One of the joys of such an activity is seeing the return during spring and summer of many old friends!)

We've had a lot of visitors that arrived here in the spring;
They didn't come by boat or car, but came here on the wing.
I'm talking of our migrant birds; there're many come to stay
Only in the warmer months, and then they fly away.

Some swifts fly in from Asia, from Siberia and Japan;
Few birds can fly as fast as them, it's catch them if you can!
Cuckoo shrikes and cuckoos fly in from northern States,
As does the welcome swallow, which you'll find is never late!

Swamp harriers which hunt on farms are others which have come
For a pleasant summer sojourn, and leave when summer's done!
And many of the fantails are visitors to here;
But some are residential, and stay throughout the year!

And from near the Arctic Circle the wading birds come in,
You'll see them on the wetlands when the warmer days begin.
Fifteen thousand K they cover and sometimes even more!
When coming from Siberia to our Tasmanian shore.

They come in hordes to visit, and on a summer's day
You'll see them on the mudflats, lagoons and reefs and bay.
Godwit, whimbrel, turnstone, greenshank, curlew, knot,
Stint and snipe and sanderling, and others I forgot!

There are others which come visiting but, like some human friends,
We find from May to August their visitations end!
But when the winter's over, we see them once again,
To enjoy their songs and presence on hill and shore and plain!

BLAME THE WEATHER!

(Don't we all?!)

My voice is all croaky,
All raspy and throaty,
You can hear I'm a little bit hoarse.
It seems many a virus
Finds us most desirous,
I didn't invite them, of course!

It's the change in the weather
That brings us together,
The germs and the viruses, too.
At some inappropriate moment,
They invade us and foment;
A savage and miserable brew!

These feisty pervaders
That love to invade us
Are fine when the weather is calm!
But bring us a gale,
Or thunder and hail,
They wake, and seek to do harm!

One day - fine and thirty,
Next day - wet and dirty,
Next morning we might have a storm.
When weather is changing,
These bugs are arranging
To visit, their strife to perform!

I'm at the end of my tether
With this changeable weather,
But the weather bureau's not to blame.
Germs wouldn't have started
This cold they've imparted,
If we'd had several days all the same!

PEACE ON THE FARM

(An idyllic dream, perhaps?)

There are ducks on the dam and an assortment of frogs,
Along with a yabby or two.
And a family of wrens are searching the logs,
With the male a magnificent blue.

They're looking for grubs in the wood that's decayed,
Which I guess makes a good deal of sense.
And most of the sheep are asleep in the shade
Of a small clump of trees by the fence.

On the hillside nearby through the shimmering haze
That distorts the pictures I see,
I can watch the black cattle all peacefully graze,
While they can look back at me!

And down in the house yard the dogs are at rest,
Curled up at the end of their chain.
The chooks are exploring the garden with zest,
For the gate's been left open again!

An eagle above, looking truly superb,
Soars high on wings that are still.
The harsh call of ravens the silence disturbs,
And the plovers join in with a will.

The mice in the haystack are waiting for night,
They rest through the hours of the day.
The cats, too, are sleeping while it is still light,
They wait for the evening to play.

Nearby, like a statue, stands Betsy, the mare,
Pondering on days that are past;
With a dozen companions she once used to share
On the farm, but now she's the last.

So all is at peace on the farm where I stay;
Well, not quite, for the farmer's about.
And he's busy, so busy through most of the day,
But all for good reason, no doubt!

He's got so much to do, so much to inspect
In the paddocks, the yard and the shed!
While all of the animals watch him and reflect
Why isn't he resting instead!

But he's off on the tractor, or driving his truck,
Or checking the pump by the creek;
Or fixing up something that's broken or stuck!
He's working near eight days a week!

There are ducks on the dam, and an assortment of frogs,
Along with a yabby or two.
And I say to myself as I sit on a log,
"Why farm? There's too much to do!"

A PROVERBIAL POEM WITH RURAL FLAVOUR!

(Some years ago one of my daughters gave me a large book entitled 'Proverbs, Sentences, and Proverbial Phrases from English Writings Mainly before 1500'. Certainly a mouthful, but a book I find fascinating! I've used some of the odd phrases and sayings from this book in this poem.)

He was bald as a cow,
And as rough as a cow;
And dressed as well as a cow wears a saddle.
She was as comely, I gauge,
As a cow in a cage,
Which nowadays is so much fiddle-faddle!

But one cannot deny,
As he cast a sheep's eye,
He was really a wolf in sheep's clothing.
Yet maids followed like sheep,
But like children, would weep,
For he wasn't what maids were behooving!

He was foul as a goat!
This wolf in sheep's coat;
And he roared like a bagged horse too often.
When he ate like a horse,
All the maidens, of course,
Lived in hope that his manner would soften.

But this fellow obtuse,
Who knew less than a goose,
And staggered like geese after drinking;
Till the end of his days
Would not change his ways,
And it's time to end this, I'm thinking!

COUNTRY SPORT

(I have spent over forty years playing sport in various rural communities. Cricket, football, badminton, table tennis, volleyball and basketball - I've played them all - and have numerous trophies to prove it! In many country areas, sport is still a vital part of community life, as I can well attest!)

For forty-odd years I played country sport,
And I didn't much mind whatever the sort
Of game that I played, but cricket was best,
Yet I really enjoyed playing all of the rest:
Table tennis, badminton, basketball, too,
And soccer and football before I was through!

Many seasons of volleyball, also, I played,
And we did pretty well, for I have displayed
A shelf full of trophies to say that we won
A fistful of finals —'A' Grade's Number One!!
But one of the best things about country sport
Is the wonderful friendship and district support!

I visit my nephew when I'm interstate,
Where I am assured of hospitality great!
He's lived on a farm for all of his life,
And so have the children, and so has his wife.
And on every Saturday there's never a doubt
They'll be off to watch sport, year in and year out.

It's a community thing; all the families attend
To watch sons and daughters, or some of their friends
As they play football or tennis, netball or cricket;
For a pleasant few hours these days are the ticket!
There's chatter and barbecues, laughter and fun,
As the district enjoy a day out in the sun!

The day starts quite early, the juniors play first,
And one finds that the fathers work up a thirst
As they cheer on their youngsters, and others do, too,
And for stubbies or cuppas there's always a queue!
But many don't queue, they bring picnics, you see,
With a thermos or two, for coffee or tea.

The community day often drifts into night,
And folk stay for tea, and usually delight
In noisy post-mortems, why they lost or they won,
And then the day ends like the day has begun
With a few friendly words, a handshake or two,
Then the following week they'll do it anew!

TOTALLY UNRIVALLED
AWESOME ARCHER
FIRST CLASS
ALL-TIME GREATEST
MOST REVERED
CHAMPION
MOST MODEST
BEST EVER
REAL GOOD
STAR
1ST RAFFIA WORK
FIRST
WINNE
SKI CLUB
CHAMPIO

ICONS???

(The use of the word 'icon' has become very popular over the past few years, with many and varied people, objects and landmarks being labelled 'Australian icons'. I've chosen a few that I think could justifiably be given such a title.)

Gloster shirts and Blundstone boots,
They're as Aussie as mallee roots.
Akubra hats and RM, too,
Australian icons through and through.
Vegemite and merino sheep,
Adam Lindsay Gordon's leap;
Sydney ferries and Melbourne trams,
Sunday's dinner – a leg of lamb!
Drovers, shearers, Jackie Howe,
Swaggies, and the stump-jump plough.
The Opera House is ridgy-didge,
As is the Sydney Harbour Bridge.
Sir Donald Bradman and Ned Kelly,
Dame Joan Sutherland and Dame Nellie;
I've heard folk say they're icons, too,
Are they iconic things to you?

HYPERTENSION

(I talked about the dangers of hypertension on the radio in Tasmania - and followed the talk with this poem!)

Hypertension! Hypertension!
It's a word that's often mentioned
In the chemist's, at the doctor's, and in hospitals each day.
Hypertension is the measure
Of high vascular blood pressure,
And it is a silent killer, and it rarely goes away!

You might think it doesn't matter
If you get a little fatter,
Or smoke a cigarette or two, or, perhaps, a large cigar.
But these smokes and fatty diet
Can often cause a riot
In our many veins and arteries, no matter who you are.

And, before you disappear,
Have you any vague idea
What your blood pressure might be reading on this pleasant Sunday
morn?
If you don't, then get it measured,
At the chemist, at your leisure,
Or on a visit to your doctor, you can't say you've not been warned!

It's a killer, hypertension,
And it's beyond my comprehension
Why some folks don't even bother to have it checked just now
and then.
For most there's medication
To relieve the situation,
So go and get it checked this week, or it may be 'aye, amen!'

MOUNT SELDOM SEEN

(What a marvellous name for a remote mountain! This poem is self-explanatory.)

In Victoria's highland country well off the beaten track
Is a mountain aptly titled Seldom Seen.
So far away from anywhere it's classified outback,
But a place where I've quite often been.

Well, 'quite often' may be stretching it, I've been there once or twice,
And I've climbed the spotter's tower at the top.
At its base there is a cabin, and a loo that will suffice
For those who may require a toilet stop!

Now this loo is just a dunny perched on a stony rise
Along a path of twenty yards or more.
And this dunny is three-sided, which for some is a surprise,
For this structure has been built without a door!

It's a little wooden building and its doorway faces east,
Leaving users with an unimpeded view
Of marvellous mountain country on which their eyes can feast,
From the confines of this low-tech highland loo!

Whether driving through the winter snow or through the summer
dust,
And you come across a track to Seldom Seen;
Just remember that a visit to that dunny is a must!
For the view from there will make you glad you've been!

2006 - WHAT WILL IT BRING?

(By the time you read this poem, 2006 may well be past and gone! But when I wrote it, 2006 was still two days away. These are my thoughts regarding the year to come.)

I was still at primary school in nineteen forty-six,
And that is when I first, I think, went to the local flicks!
The United Nations, too, was formed - and George Bush and his
wife,
As well as William Clinton, saw their first year of life.

There're some events in fifty-six I never will forget,
The Olympic Games in Melbourne; they are with me yet!
Another highlight of that year was black-and-white TV;
But I had to go to uncle's house for shows I wished to see!

And sixty-six was special, too, the year my wife and I
Started on our married life - the thirteenth of July!
And earlier on, in February, a major change occurred,
We switched to decimal currency, which some thought quite absurd!

Agatha Christie died in seventy-six, and so did Chairman Mao.
So many mysteries Christie wrote, I really don't know how!
Our youngest daughter, too, was born, the final one of four,
And now the grandkids that we have number even more!

Disasters struck in eighty-six, and many felt the pain!
There was a nuclear meltdown in Chernobyl in Ukraine;
The space shuttle exploded, and other troubles, too,
But in our starry heavens, Halley's comet came in view.

John Howard became prime minister in nineteen ninety-six,
It seems to be for ever that he's been in politics!
The first cloned sheep was Dolly, though few there were could
pick it!
And Sri Lanka beat Australia in the grand World Cup of cricket.

Two double 0 six is waiting, it comes in just two days,
Will it be a spluttering candle? Or set the world ablaze?
Regardless of what happens, take one day at a time,
I wish you each a great new year as I end this rhyme!

MUSEUMS

(I love museums! I love to see the artefacts of past civilisations, to see the natural wonders of this amazing world, and so forth. Nowadays, however, some of the items are somewhat familiar!)

Museums are a favourite place to while the time away,
To see the common things of life of ancient yesterdays.
To see the strange and beautiful, to see the quite bizarre,
To appreciate the 'how they were', and not the 'how they are'!
See how our forebears lived and worked in some past yesteryear,
To see the trinkets, toys and jewels our ancestors held dear.
To gaze at minerals from the mines, see bones of beasts long gone,
To see old cars and books and coins; the list goes on and on!
But what intrigues me most of all, and startles me somewhat,
Is when I see some proud display of many things I've got!

BESS, THE BLACK ORPINGTON SWAGGIE

(This is the only poem in this book that has been published before. Bess is the heroine of a novel I wrote in 1993 called "Bess the Black Orpington Swaggie". The story is about two swaggies who travel around outback Australia in the late 1940's. It just so happens that one of the swaggies is Bess the talking chook!)

She was raised on a farm in Dimboola, surrounded by Wimmera
wheat;
She knew icy frosts in the winter, she suffered the long summer's
heat.
A little, black Orpington chicken, she grew to a good-laying hen,
But her thoughts often turned to adventure, away from her wire-
netting pen.

Each morning the farmer's son, Arthur, would let her out into the
yard,
Along with the rest of the layers, (for whom she had little regard);
For Bess, as this Arthur had named her, was a tough, independent,
young chook,
And she'd spend many hours gazing westward, with a dreamy,
faraway look.

"My future is not as a layer, I'm sure there are more sights to see
That I could ever imagine, and the life on the road is for me."
So she gathered a few, basic items, wrapped up in a calico bag;
And tied the bag up in a blanket - a little, black Orpington's swag.

Thereafter each night she would settle, not in with the rest of the
hens,
But under the cart on the axle, for this was the means to her ends;
At last came the night she was wanting, the family went out in the
cart;
As she bumped along on the axle, excitement rose high in her
heart.

The family was off to tin-kettle a young couple who'd recently
wed,
And they waited, of course, till they reckoned the couple would
be well in bed;
So off in the darkness they trotted, unaware that Black Bess
underneath,
Was having a ride - had she had them - that would loosen all of
her teeth!

So the couple was duly tin-kettled; then Arthur discovered the hen -
"Hey! Look!" he exclaimed, most astonished, "Black Bess has
got out of her pen!"
'Twas then that Black Bess nearly panicked, but she kept her
swag hidden from view;
And Arthur said, "Might as well leave her, she looks like she's
stuck on with glue!"

When they'd finished tin-kettling the couple, they all drifted back
to their homes,
The Gardiner's, the Smith's, and the Griffiths'; the Shepherd's,
the Menzies' and Baume's.
But Black Bess never reached the old farmhouse, she jumped off
at the road leading west:
With her swag, with its blanket and billy - she started her journey
with zest.

Through the small hours of morning she plodded, and then, at the breaking of day,
They saw her nearing Jeparit, two travellers from over Perth way:
No longer a jaunty, young chicken, her feet were now blistered and raw;
And she'd wrapped them up in blue denim, to stop them feeling so sore.

One of the travellers stopped her, and spoke with a voice kind and true,
"And what are you doing, young chicken? And where are you travelling to?"
But Bessie could not speak too clearly, and the one word that she answered back
Was a feebly drawn-out husky "Arthur" as she stumbled along on the track.

There was drought in the wheat belt that summer, and meals were a problem each day,
But she worked her way all round the country, from Quilpie, to Wentworth and Hay.
She swept up the crutchings in woolsheds, she helped press the wool into bales,
She even helped out with the muster, way out in west New South Wales.

She trampled through the year 'forty-seven, the year of the Mallee
mouse plague,
She remembered it all very clearly, though my recollections are
vague.
She ate rabbit stew with the swaggies, and often repaid with an
egg;
For an Orpington proud was young Bessie, she'd vowed she'd
not steal food or beg.

After two or three years in the outback, she headed for different
terrain;
It was up in the mountains I met her, with the cattle up on the
high plain.
She told me she often missed Arthur, to Dimboola one day she'd
return;
But she still had a sense of adventure, she still had a lot more to
learn.

By now she was really quite famous, Black Bess the Orpington
chook;
And the shearers and drovers all knew her, she was often
employed as their cook.
She learnt to play fiddle and banjo; and many a station outback,
Would ask her to play at their dances each time she blew in from
The Track.

She travelled from Wave Hill to Derby, and then on to Kimberley
Downs.
She travelled all over Australia, keeping out of the really big
towns.
For some years I heard nothing of her; I thought she by then
must have died,
But late in the fifties I saw her, there was no mistaking her stride.

I pulled up beside her and chatted, and, strike me! She knew me
by name,
This now battered, old, greying Bessie, still plucky, courageous
and game.
She still had her bluey and billy, the same that she'd taken that
day
From the kitchen she'd known as a chicken, when she lived over
Dimboola way.

She said, with a voice sounding weary, she'd now had enough of
The Track,
With the flies, and the dust, and the tourists - "too many now
travel outback."
She said that she'd do one more circuit - to say fond goodbyes to
her friends,
Then settle back home in Dimboola, with Arthur and some of his
hens.

And so we are now in the nineties, I've not seen old Bess now for
years,
But sometimes, when oldies are chatting, I a rumour occasionally
hears
About a black Orpington swaggie they'd met somewhere out on
The Track;
But I doubt that I'll e'er again see her, I doubt that she'll ever
come back.

SPIDERS! - MILLIONS OF SPIDERS!

(Why is it that spiders are among the least liked of all living creatures? Is it their eight legs? Is it their reputation for inflicting nasty wounds? Is it the mess they make with their webs? Or is it simply they are everywhere - inside and outside our house!)

I remember reading somewhere in a book long years ago
About our spider population - you wouldn't want to know
How many there are living in an acre of our land,
Whether mountain, plain or suburb, whether bush or desert sand,
There are millions every acre! That's not a pretty thought!
So many spiders everywhere! And hardly any caught!

When we've got that many spiders, then it means that in each home,
Both in the house and its surroundings, a million of them roam
Unnoticed and untroubled, except for those we see;
Where all the rest are hiding is a puzzling mystery!
Although, when I think about it, we can often see the signs
In the cobwebs all about us, and their intricate designs.

You can sweep the cobwebs daily, but next day you'll find them
        back;
In the yard I notice hundreds as I walk the garden track!
And you fellows, take a gander at the cobwebs in your shed,
They're there in every corner, on the bench and overhead!
You'll find them in the garage, you'll find them on the car,
You can even find a cobweb in your unused steel guitar!

Inside the house you'll find them, and you'll see the spiders, too,
I've seen spiders in the shower, I've seen them swimming in the loo!
They hide behind the pictures that are hanging on the wall,
I've seen them large and hairy, I've seen them colourful and small.
I've seen them in the kitchen sink, I've seen them in the bed,
And I know a lot of people only like them when they're dead!

I've swept cobwebs off the rafters, and behind our many doors,
I've swept cobwebs off the windows, and from cupboards and
        from drawers;
I've found spiders in the wood box, I've found spiders in my boots;
I've found spiders scared and timid, and I've chased aggressive
        brutes!
I've found them underneath the chairs and on the laundry shelf;
I reckon if I slept too long I'd find them on myself!

CHOOKS

(Regardless of what 'proper' name they may have, most Australians will call domestic fowl, chooks!)

If you're a poultry farmer you've probably heard the name
Of that ornamental chicken that's called Old English Game.
A descendant of the fighting cock, unlike the Delaware,
That's a dual-purpose chicken from America somewhere.
It's white and rapid-growing, and the eggs it lays are brown,
As are the eggs of Orpingtons from some old Kentish town.
The Orpington's a heavy bird, and popular with cooks;
But we're not into fancy names, us Aussies call them chooks.

A very tasty chicken, or so I've heard it said,
Is another breed from USA, the plump New Hampshire Red.
They're fairly new, as fowl breeds go, unlike the bird Malay;
Which is an ancient Asian fowl from some far yesterday.
Then there's the Jersey Giant, a quite outstanding sight!
Weighing up to thirteen pounds, it can be black or white.
But despite their size or heritage, regardless of their looks,
I'm sure, that if we saw them, we'd simply call them chooks!

Barnevelders come from Holland, a dual-purpose breed,
As is the Dorking chicken; its legs are short indeed!
From China comes the Silkie, a fluffy, little bird,
Whose different type of feathers makes it look a touch absurd!
The Australorp's Australian, and produces many eggs;
And the Andalusian's Spanish, with long and sturdy legs.
But no matter where their home is, be it London or Tobruk;
Once venturing to Australia they'll each be known as chook!